Freedom, Common Sense, and the "Nanny State"

Also by Richard T. Stanley, Ed.D.

Lessons of American History
A Humorous Account of America's Past: 986 to 1898
A Humorous Account of America's Past: 1898 to 1945
A Humorous Account of America's Past: 1945 to 2001
The Eisenhower Years: A Social History of the 1950's
The Psychedelic Sixties: A Social History of the 1960's

Freedom, Common Sense, and the "Nanny State"

Richard T. Stanley

iUniverse, Inc.
Bloomington

Freedom, Common Sense, and the "Nanny State"

iUniverse books may be ordered through booksellers or by contacting:

iUniverse
1663 Liberty Drive
Bloomington, IN 47403
www.iuniverse.com
1-800-Authors (1-800-288-4677)

ISBN: 978-1-4759-7430-0 (sc)
ISBN: 978-1-4759-7431-7 (ebk)

Printed in the United States of America

iUniverse rev. date: 02/04/2013

Freedom, Common Sense, and the "Nanny State"

Richard T. Stanley

iUniverse, Inc.
Bloomington

Freedom, Common Sense, and the "Nanny State"

iUniverse books may be ordered through booksellers or by contacting:

iUniverse
1663 Liberty Drive
Bloomington, IN 47403
www.iuniverse.com
1-800-Authors (1-800-288-4677)

Because of the dynamic nature of the Internet, any web addresses or links contained in this book may have changed since publication and may no longer be valid. The views expressed in this work are solely those of the author and do not necessarily reflect the views of the publisher, and the publisher hereby disclaims any responsibility for them.

Any people depicted in stock imagery provided by Thinkstock are models, and such images are being used for illustrative purposes only. Certain stock imagery © Thinkstock.

ISBN: 978-1-4759-7430-0 (sc)
ISBN: 978-1-4759-7431-7 (ebk)

Printed in the United States of America

iUniverse rev. date: 02/04/2013

Table of Contents

DEDICATION

This book is dedicated to all individuals who love freedom, have common sense, and loathe the "Nanny State."

PREFACE

I began writing, *Freedom, Common Sense, and the "Nanny State"* the morning after President Barack Obama was reelected. I was saddened by America's choice at the polls. But I was not shocked. The Election of 2012 was one of the most divisive national elections in American history. Not since the Election of 1828—General Andrew Jackson vs. President John Quincy Adams—has character assassination played so great a role. During the campaign, Republicans claimed President Obama acted like a malevolent (and possibly foreign-born) Santa Claus who wasted precious tax dollars on "Stimulus" boondoggles and bogus "investments"—*and worse*. Democrats cleverly countered by characterizing Governor Romney as a 21st Century Ebenezer Scrooge who hated the bottom forty-seven percent of Americans, and as a man who would not hesitate to push ol' grandma over the edge of a cliff (or deprive Tiny Tim of his crutch) just to save a buck. On election day, a slim majority of voters chose Santa Claus over Ebenezer Scrooge. Their decision, if unfortunate for our nation's financial future, was certainly understandable. *Santa or Scrooge?*

So now what should we loyal Americans do? That is precisely why I wrote this book.

Richard T. Stanley, Ed.D.
Long Beach, California

PREFACE

I began writing, *Freedom, Common Sense, and the "Nanny State"* the morning after President Barack Obama was reelected. I was saddened by America's choice at the polls. But I was not shocked. The Election of 2012 was one of the most divisive national elections in American history. Not since the Election of 1828—General Andrew Jackson vs. President John Quincy Adams—has character assassination played so great a role. During the campaign, Republicans claimed President Obama acted like a malevolent (and possibly foreign-born) Santa Claus who wasted precious tax dollars on "Stimulus" boondoggles and bogus "investments"—*and worse*. Democrats cleverly countered by characterizing Governor Romney as a 21st Century Ebenezer Scrooge who hated the bottom forty-seven percent of Americans, and as a man who would not hesitate to push ol' grandma over the edge of a cliff (or deprive Tiny Tim of his crutch) just to save a buck. On election day, a slim majority of voters chose Santa Claus over Ebenezer Scrooge. Their decision, if unfortunate for our nation's financial future, was certainly understandable. *Santa or Scrooge*?

So now what should we loyal Americans do? That is precisely why I wrote this book.

Richard T. Stanley, Ed.D.
Long Beach, California

Chapter 1

....

DEFICIT SPENDING

Since the fall of 2008, we Americans have experienced an ongoing financial crisis of a greater magnitude than any economic recession in our nation's history since the Great Depression of the 1930's. Since 2008, times have been tough. Unemployment has been unusually high. Real estate values have fallen. Housing and commercial construction have declined. Bankruptcy rates have risen. Credit has tightened and the availability of bank loans has shrunk. Imports have continued to exceed exports. Low interest rates have discouraged savings accounts. Manufacturing, once the leading sector of America's economic growth during the 1940's, '50's, and '60's, has largely moved overseas. Fortunately, our nation's farms continue to produce far more food than we can consume here at home. But agribusiness employs fewer farm families than ever before due to increasing consolidation and modern production methods.

Since the fall of 2008, the average American family's annual income has significantly declined, while the incomes of Wall Street executives and professional athletes have skyrocketed. If you disagree, name *one* major league baseball star who currently earns a lower annual salary than the President of the United States.

So, what should we do to end our nation's growing debt? And how should we proceed? First, our political leaders must admit that they have a *spending problem*. This is not a partisan issue; it's simply a *fact*. One thing is mathematically certain: We Americans can no longer sustain our federal government's current spending levels by simply raising taxes on the rich. Or, for that matter, by raising *everyone's* taxes. The days of kicking the can down the fiscal highway for some future generation to worry about are over, *kaput*!

More specifically, how have we arrived at the edge of this gigantic financial abyss, this so-called "Fiscal Cliff"? Just blaming Bush II will not suffice. The roots of our overspending go as far back as the 1970's. In my view, America's ongoing fiscal crisis—whether it involves our federal government in Washington, D.C., or such financially overextended states as California, Illinois, and New York—is a manifestation of a larger and more all-encompassing culture war, *Self-reliance vs. "Social Justice."* Americans who seek a more self-reliant society generally prefer individual responsibility, entrepreneurship, and limited government. Americans who seek a more cooperative society generally advocate "social justice," "shared wealth," and an expansive government. Most Americans in *either* ideological camp have noble intentions. But noble intentions that become laws without the necessary means to pay for them can lead to financial ruin. Folks, the old bromide, *There is no free lunch!*, still holds true. Someone eventually pays.

Historically, America's philosophy of self-reliance and limited government is based on our Founding Father's beliefs—especially those of Thomas Jefferson and James Madison. Their thoughts regarding individual freedom and limited government were soon eloquently bolstered by

Ralph Waldo Emerson's *transcendentalism*—the once revolutionary notion that there is some nobility in each individual and in all work. Emerson extolled the virtues of "Self-reliance," and the world took notice.

"Social Justice," or the "rights" of less-fortunate Americans to certain government-granted "entitlements," is a more recent phenomena in our history. The granting of tax dollars in the form of jobs, cash, food, clothing, and/or shelter as "entitlements" to the poor and handicapped first proliferated with the expansion of our federal government during President Franklin D. Roosevelt's New Deal as part of his efforts to cope with the Great Depression of the 1930's. Most of FDR's social justice programs of the 1930's required their recipients to perform some sort of work (such as in the CCC or the WPA), or to contribute financially (Social Security). Most social justice programs of the 1930's required each recipient to qualify by *doing or giving something of value*. While radical for its time, the New Deal was not free *welfare*.

Fast forward to the last decade of the 20th Century. On December 25, 1991, with the sudden, dramatic, and highly ironic collapse of the God-less

Soviet Union on the most holy of Christian holidays, America became the world's only superpower. We Americans suddenly found ourselves in the catbird seat. We had finally won the Cold War. Fears of a nuclear Armageddon dissolved. *Pax Americana* was ours to savor. Life was sweet.

In the Election of 1992, President George H.W. Bush's recent victory in the first Gulf War was trumped at the polls by Arkansas Governor Bill Clinton's more progressive, peacetime domestic proposals. (Do you remember Clinton's winning slogan, "It's the ECONOMY, stupid!"?) With the demise of what former President Ronald Reagan chose to call "The Evil Empire," domestic matters during the Clinton Administration quickly took center stage as a new era of "normalcy" began. During the Clinton Years, given a fiscally conservative Congress whose "Contract with America" required smaller and smarter federal spending within the confines of a *balanced budget*, the United States Treasury actually built up a surplus.

As we Americans focused primarily on our domestic economy during the Clinton Years, festering social issues bubbled to the surface. Chief among them were three volatile topics, the so-called "Three G's of modern American politics"—Gays,

5

Guns, and God. Taken together, these three "hot-button" issues tended to divide our two major political parties into opposing camps for moral, rather than fiscal, reasons. Republicans generally campaigned on "family values," the "right-to-life," and the "right to bear arms." Democrats, on the other hand, increasingly advocated "gay rights," the "right-to-choose," and "gun control." Opposing stands by politicians and their supporters regarding these highly-emotional, "hot-buttons" issues gave rise to a more curt and partisan political culture in America. Political discourse between Democrats and Republicans grew increasingly hostile. And, while the continuing arguments over gays, guns, and God did not cause our federal government to overspend, they certainly contributed to an atmosphere in the halls of Congress and elsewhere of growing non-cooperation.

The impeachment of President Clinton by the Republican-led House of Representatives in 1998 made America's political climate even more heated. But angry partisanship reached its peak following the Disputed Election of 2000 (which had ironically proven to be a rather lackluster presidential campaign between "Gush and Bore") as the vote-counting and recounting fiasco in Florida dragged on and on. Americans took sides. Tempers flared. Neither side trusted the other. Armies of attorneys for each side descended upon Florida. The U.S. Supreme Court had to finally settle the matter by a five to four vote. George Bush became our forty-third president under a cloud of suspicion: Did the Republicans steal the election?

The shock of America's second Pearl Harbor on September 11, 2001, instantly galvanized Americans into a singleness of purpose. The horrific and unprovoked attack by a band of Islamic extremists on the Twin Towers in New York City and the Pentagon in our nation's capital brought Americans together behind our new Commander-in-Chief with one patriotic purpose: *Seek and destroy the bastards who were responsible for masterminding the slaughter of over 3,000 innocent Americans!*

First, we sought them in Afghanistan, then in Iraq. Destroying the Afghan militias and the Iraqi army in direct combat soon proved far easier than managing our subsequent occupation of both countries and our "nation building" efforts in each. American casualties continued. Costs soared. Congress began to deficit spend again, big time. Some Americans grumbled, but nearly all continued to support our troops. Our fighting men and women, in fact, were more honored than at any time since World War II. Unfortunately, our national debt continued to grow into the trillions of dollars. But neither political party in the Congress risked making serious cuts in military spending and/ or entitlements. (After all, our *first* trillion dollars in debt, without compounded interest, would only cost every man, woman, and child in the United States a little more than $3,000 *each*. So, not to worry.) During the Bush Years, debt, in the midst of prosperity, became the new normal.

The sudden Recession of 2008, brought on, in part, by greedy and shoddy loan practices and inflated home prices that led to an avalanche of defaults on home mortgages, hit Wall Street like a ton of bricks. Several major financial houses closed their doors. People panicked. Banks reduced their lines of credit for Main Street businesses. Jobs were lost. Sales fell. More jobs were lost. Those still employed in the private sector faced likely reductions in wages and benefits. Our federal government seemed almost powerless to stop the economic bleeding. Meanwhile, government expenditures continued to exceed revenues at a growing rate. The United States of America, the world's leading creditor nation since World War I, was rapidly *going broke*. Only continued foreign investment in U.S. Treasury securities, especially by China, Japan, and Brazil, plus currency manipulations by our Federal Reserve, kept us afloat.

In the midst of the financial panic, a national election was held. Our new president, Illinois Senator Barack Obama, won on his promise of "Hope and Change." In early 2009, with President Obama's full approval, the Democrat-led House and Senate dusted off the 1930's economic theories of the famous British economist John Maynard Keynes. Keynes believed that only increased government spending could compensate for insufficient private investment during times of economic recession. FDR used Keynes's ideas during the Great Depression in his attempts to prop-up America's economy through government assistance. FDR often described his increased federal spending to the American public back then as "priming the pump." President Obama, recognizing that few Americans still pumped water from their own wells, publicly described his Keynes-based answer to the recession as his "Economic Stimulus Package." Old theory, new language.

9

Most historians now agree that America's economy was even worse in 1937, FDR's fifth year in office, than it was in 1933, the fourth year of the Great Depression and Roosevelt's first year as president, having replaced a dishonored Herbert Hoover following the Election of 1932. Unfortunately, it took World War II, which began in Europe in September 1939, not Keynesian economics, to pull us out of our financial doldrums. Will the Obama Administration's Keynesian-style stimulus policies ultimately produce better results than FDR's past efforts? Or, God help us all, must we hope for some sort of World War III to bail us out? (Or eliminate us entirely.)

Seriously, let's look at a few facts. First, President Obama has piled up more debt to date than *all of our previous forty-three presidents COMBINED!* Second, with President Obama's reelection in 2012, *"social justice" and big government* have again triumphed in the culture war against *self-reliance and limited government.* Third, our total national debt now exceeds *sixteen trillion* dollars. If a mere trillion dollars in debt without compounded interest amounts to more than $3,000 owed by every American man, woman, and child (the $3,000 does *not* include on-going local, state, and federal taxes and fees), imagine for one frightening moment how much each of us now owes on over $16,400,000,000,000 in national debt *with interest*. Fourth, the costs of our federal entitlement programs—Social Security, Medicare, unemployment insurance, food stamps, housing assistance for the poor and handicapped, etc.—will surely continue to grow as the Affordable Health Care Act, a.k.a. "Obama Care," kicks in in 2014, insuring roughly thirty million additional Americans at public expense. And fifth, after considering facts one through four, our oft-disparaged friends in Greece, when compared to us, may soon be in better shape.

So, what should we do? And how should we proceed? Certainly, our federal government could use more revenue. What *family* couldn't use more income? But, in the long run, governments, like families, must try to live within their means. How much longer can our federal government spend roughly eleven billion dollars *per day* while taking in approximately five billion? Such an astounding daily deficit in income versus spending should frighten the wits out of all but the brain dead. So we Americans must all rise up as one—Democrats, Republicans, and Independents—and demand that our elected *representatives* come together and compromise on long-term spending cuts across the *entire* spectrum of federal programs—from welfare to national defense—before it is too late. Their continued failure to work together—liberals, moderates, and conservatives—in search of long-term solutions to our financial woes will soon cause America to become a land of poverty and anarchy (or dictatorship) rather than shared wealth and social justice. Liberal Americans can, and so far *are* winning the culture war *Self-reliance vs. "Social Justice."* But, to blindly continue on our current course can only lead to a pyric victory that will end in a cataclysmic collapse. We Americans must exercise common sense, reorder our priorities, and limit government spending or the America we all know and love will surely perish from this earth.

Chapter 2

. . . .

NATIONAL DEFENSE

So where should we reduce our federal spending? Spending on national defense has long been a so-called "sacred cow" for most Republicans. Republicans are certainly correct whenever they reaffirm the truism that *the basic purpose of government is protection*. Historically, most Democrats have also agreed. But anyone's sacred cow can become antiquated and bloated overtime—especially when it comes to something so essential to our republic as preparing for and maintaining our national defense. No right-minded American wants to be caught unprepared for an enemy attack. And, it is human nature to assume that *more* is always better than *less*. Certainly, weakness in our ever-dangerous world is never a viable option, especially for the United States in its role as defender of the Free World. As a result, our army generals are seldom satisfied with their allotted numbers of troops and tanks. Our navy's admirals seldom see their fleets of carriers and submarines as sufficient in number for a two-ocean conflict. And our air force generals usually request additional well-trained pilots and more-advanced attack aircraft on a regular basis in order to be properly armed and prepared to successfully meet the challenges of any possible military scenario. As with any giant bureaucracy, growth (and waste), without external constraint, is a given.

Following the end of World War II and the onset of our Cold War with the Soviet Union (and further prodded by the fall of Nationalist China to the Communists under Mao Tse-Tung in 1949), President Harry Truman adopted a national defense strategy for the United States that was *defensive* in nature and called for the *containment* of Communist aggression by committing American ground troops (such as he ordered to Korea) to whatever trouble spots arose in the world. Truman, a Democrat, began spending enormous sums of federal tax dollars once again on national defense.

14

During the Korean War, many Americans came to label Democrats as belonging to "The War Party."

When General Dwight D. Eisenhower became our thirty-fourth President following the Election of 1952, he secretly threatened the Communist Chinese that he would drop atomic bombs on China if they continued to wage war in Korea against American and UN forces.[1] By 1953, Ike, the former commander of the largest amphibious invasion force in the history of the world, had come to the conclusion that America's military was too bloated and costly. Ike believed Truman's strategy of *containing* Communist aggression by deploying large numbers of American G.I.'s in various trouble spots around the globe was inefficient and unnecessarily bloody (by then, the Korean War alone was responsible for more than 130,000 dead, wounded, or missing Americans), as well as a continuous drain on our economy. According to the former general, *more* could be accomplished with *less*—provided that America's vast stockpile of already existing nuclear weapons became a key part of our defense strategy. Ike, an expert

---

[1]   See Jim Newton's *Eisenhower: The White House Years* (New York: Doubleday, 2011), pp. 77-84.

15

poker and bridge player most of his life, knew from personal experience how to bluff an opponent to his advantage.[2] President Eisenhower strongly believed that America's trump card in the Cold War was her nuclear capability to obliterate any enemy, including the Soviet Union and Communist China, at any time within hours.

President Eisenhower had personally met many of the highest ranking Russians, including Stalin, while serving as the Commander of Allied Forces in Europe during World War II, and as the first Commander of NATO, stationed in Paris, following the war. In his keen judgment of human nature, Ike saw the Soviet Union's rulers as ruthless, but not *suicidal*. The Soviets reacted to weakness like sharks in bloody water. But, as realists, they respected *and feared* America's nuclear weapons capability, especially after Eisenhower ordered the U.S. Air Force Strategic Air Command (SAC), during the first year of his presidency, to maintain long-range B-52 bombers, armed with *atomic bombs*, on constant 24-hour alert. In addition,

---

[2]   See Evan Thomas's *Ike's Bluff: President Eisenhower's Secret Battle to Save the World* (New York: Little, Brown and Company, 2012).

Ike had Admiral Hyman Rickover's new fleet of nuclear-powered submarines, armed with atomic weapons, lurking in the oceans of the world, ready to strike with deadly force when ordered to do so.

In the minds of the leaders of the Soviet Union, what American president, when provoked, was more likely than Eisenhower to actually use nuclear weapons against them than the former Allied commander who had supervised the total destruction of Nazi Germany? And that was exactly what President Eisenhower wanted the men in the Kremlin to think. Likewise, in the case of the Communist Chinese, following Ike's secret threat to drop atomic bombs north of the Yalu River unless the Red army stopped fighting in Korea, Chairman Mao blinked, and an armistice was soon signed.

President Eisenhower also knew from his study of Clausewitz that small wars should be avoided whenever possible.[3] Small wars, according to that famous German general and military strategist, too often grow out of control and can produce unanticipated consequences that can weaken, or

---

[3]   See Stephen E. Ambrose's *Eisenhower: Soldier and President* (New York: Simon & Schuster, 1991), pp. 246-7.

17

eventually destroy, even the greatest of nations. Therefore, rather than authorize direct military involvement in trouble spots around the globe, as Truman had been wont to do, Eisenhower secretly approved deadly CIA-led covert operations in the interest of "national security" to *destabilize* Third World countries with anti-American leaders (such as Muhammad Mossadegh in Iran and Jacobo Arbenz in Guatemala) by using local, CIA-trained nationals as "patriots." Ike cut defense costs and saved American lives by using Latin-Americans against Latin-Americans, Persians against Persians, Asians against Asians, Arabs against Arabs, and Africans against Africans in local "revolutions," or "coups." Following the end of the Korean War in July 1953, no American solider was officially killed in combat during President Eisenhower's remaining seven-and-one-half years in office. Ike managed to do more with less, often in secret. And he kept America safe. Machiavelli would have approved of Ike's manipulations. And Sun Tzu, who extolled the virtues of patience and subtilty over anger and aggression when he long ago wrote in his *Art of War*, *"Ultimate excellence lies not in winning every battle but in defeating the enemy without ever fighting,"*[4] would have quietly nodded his head and smiled in agreement.

World War II ended in 1945. In 1989, the Soviet Union lost most of its "Evil Empire"—her "Iron Curtain" countries in Eastern Europe—in shocking and rapid succession as the communist regimes of Hungary (January), Poland (June), East Germany (October), Bulgaria (November), Czechoslovakia and Romania (December) collapsed in favor of Western-style democracy like a row of dominos.[5] In 1991, Russia's own Mikhail Gorbachev was forced into retirement as the old Soviet Union itself became history on Christmas Day. It seems that this succession of historic milestones should raise numerous questions relevant to today, including the following: In 2013, why does the United States still maintain a garrison of approximately 54,000 military personnel in Germany? Russia now has

---

[4] As quoted by Henry Kissinger in his excellent book, *On China* (New York: The Penguin Press, 2011), p. 28.

[5] In one of the greatest ironies in world history, America's leaders, including Truman, Eisenhower, Kennedy, Johnson, and Nixon, had long worried about the "domino theory"—a loss of one country to *Communism* could lead to the loss of others in quick succession. It finally happened—*to the Russians.*

a smaller military than India or North Korea. True, Russia still has nuclear weapons. But have the Russians become *more suicidal* since Eisenhower's time? Ronald Reagan often remarked, with tongue-in-cheek, that "The closest thing to eternal life is a government program." Does Reagan's statement hold true regarding America's continuing massive military presence in Germany?

According to recent Defense Department statistics, the United States currently accounts for approximately forty-three percent of the world's total military expenditures. We Americans pay more tax dollars for our military programs than China, Great Britain, France, Russia, Japan, Saudi Arabia, Germany, and Italy *combined*. True, protection is (or should be) the basic purpose of government. And yes, as long as Americans retain our missionary world view that we are obligated to spread our exceptional values to every part of the world, and to protect our friends from the enemies of freedom, we will continue to pay dearly. But aren't there some places we can cut military spending by doing *more* with *less*? God help us all if the answer is *no!*

To make our financial nightmare even worse, here is a far more frightening question: Did you know that our nation's enormous military spending accounts for less than twenty percent of our annual federal expenditures? *Protection*, as measured by dollars spent, is no longer the *real* basic purpose of our federal government. Providing "entitlements," such as Social Security and separate retirement benefits for federal employees, *is*.

Chapter 3

. . . .

SOCIAL SECURITY

Social Security—the role of the federal government in providing income and services to Americans who retire, are unemployed, become ill, or are disabled—has become an even greater political "sacred cow" with the American public than our need for national defense. National defense accounts for slightly less than twenty percent of our annual federal expenditures. Social Security payments alone amount to over twenty percent of our annual federal spending. And, when spending on such related "safety net" programs as *Medicare* (13% of our budget and growing), "*Health*" (another 11%), including health care services, "*Income Security*" (a whopping 18%), including *federal employee retirement and disability payments*, housing assistance, and food and nutrition assistance, and *Veterans Benefits and Services* (3%), including income security and hospital and medical care for veterans, are combined with Social Security payments, our federal government's growing umbrella of social assistance programs equaled an eye-popping *forty-five percent* of our total federal spending in 2010, according to the U.S. Office of Management and Budget. And, as more so-called "baby-boomers" retire, the total cost of federal entitlements, in terms of both percentages and actual dollars, continues to *increase.*

According to our federal government's official budget figures for the year 2010, our nation's total income ("net receipts") was $2,162,724,000,000. That same year, 2010, our federal government's spending ("outlays") totaled $3,456,213,000,000. Budgeting is simple math, not rocket science. For the year 2010, subtract outlays (the money we spent) of $3.456 trillion from our net receipts (the money we collected from individual income taxes, corporate income taxes, Social Security taxes and other retirement taxes, excise taxes, federal trust fund taxes, and other receipts) of $2.162 trillion, and you end up with *minus $1.294 trillion*—the amount you (we) still owe someone (China?). *Plus interest*, because even our Treasury Department isn't entitled to a free lunch. As anyone with a home mortgage, a car loan, and/or credit card debt can tell you, interest can really add up over time.

How did we Americans allow ourselves to get into this fiscal mess of owing over sixteen trillion dollars in debt? We can continue to blame former President George Bush for turning a $236 billion federal surplus for the year 2000 that he inherited from the Clinton Administration into a $318 billion deficit for the year 2005 alone. We can blame two costly foreign conflicts as part of our "War on Terror," one in Afghanistan and the other in Iraq. We can certainly blame President Barack Obama for piling up more federal debt *than all of our previous forty-three presidents COMBINED* since he assumed office in January 2009. We can even blame the Chinese and, to a lesser extent, the Japanese and the Brazilians (and other foreigners) for manufacturing most of the goods we purchase and for holding so much of our national debt in the form of U.S. Treasury securities. But what good will all that blame accomplish? Bush is retired. Obama was reelected in 2012 in spite of his miserable record on the economy. And frankly, thank God the

Chinese, the Japanese, the Brazilians, and other foreigners are still willing to hold on to most of their U.S. Treasury securities instead of cashing them in. No, while we still have First Amendment rights to blame anyone whom we choose for our fiscal mess, I suggest that we consult the wisdom of an old newspaper cartoon for kids and the young at heart—*Pogo*. As a very wise Pogo once said, "We have met the enemy, and it is *us!*" *We* bought their campaign promises to fix things. *We* trusted them to spend OUR TAX DOLLARS wisely. Now, *we* must search for practical solutions and demand that they are implemented.

So, where should *we* start? I suggest we start with some plain old elementary school math as it applies to interest rates. Interest rates are currently at all-time lows. History tells us they will not stay low for long. What if they should eventually return to the levels that existed during President Jimmy Carter's Administration during the late 1970's? During the late 1970's, interest rates on home mortgages, for example, were roughly *five times* (closer to today's credit card rates) higher than they are today. Back then, the typical interest rate for a new, fixed-rate mortgage ranged from 15% to 17%. An $80,000 loan at 17% ended up costing the borrower a total of $281,628 during the life of the loan. The borrower eventually paid back $80,000 *plus* $201,628 (or refinanced when interest rates came down). That same loan amount of $80,000 at 12% for a fixed-rate twenty-year loan cost $880.87 per month instead of the 17% loan's monthly rate of $1,173.45. Nevertheless, on an $80,000 fixed-rate twenty-year loan at 12%, the borrower still owed the bank a whopping $131,408.80 EXTRA.

If our current national debt stays at "only" sixteen-plus trillion dollars (and it will most likely *increase daily*), imagine what the actual cost *with interest* will be for us, our children, and for our children's children—especially when our low interest rates begin to rise? It has already been estimated by some economists that every man, woman, and child in America currently owes more than $110,000 on our unpaid national debt. Is this the future we want for ourselves, our children, and our children's children? Recently, President Obama smiled at the TV cameras and asked his fellow Americans to "Look Forward." Is our cataclysmic national debt due to Presidential and Congressional mismanagement really something that any of us who have some sanity remaining truly can look *forward* to? Far better that *we* convince our neighbors and our Representatives in Congress, including our do-nothing Senate, that federal spending must be reduced dramatically *now*. No one wants to push grandma off the cliff in her wheelchair. But the grandma we all love will likely not even have a wheelchair in which to be pushed if we do not as a nation act swiftly to cut spending. Failure to act appropriately will soon force *all* Americans over the fiscal cliff—including our wheelchair-less grandmas—into the abyss of another Great Depression. We must make cuts in national defense and Social Security—*including "Income Security" federal employee retirement benefits. And foreign aid.*

Chapter 4

. . . .

FOREIGN AID

By 2010, our federal government was already going broke. In addition to our previous annual (and cumulative) federal deficits, including the Bush Administration's shortfall of $318.3 billion in 2005, $160.7 billion in 2007, and in 2008, after the collapse of several major financial institutions supposedly "too big to let fail," $458.5 billion, by 2010, anxious Americans began to peer at the so-called "debt clock" and scratch their heads in amazement. One fact few Americans knew in 2010, as our national debt continued to skyrocket under President Obama, was that America's total expenditures for "International Affairs," including *foreign aid*, had increased approximately 163% in just ten years.

During President Bill Clinton's last year in office, America's total federal expenditures for "international Affairs," including international development and humanitarian assistance, international security assistance, the conduct of foreign affairs, and foreign information and exchange activities, totaled $17.213 billion. By the end of 2010, America's spending on international affairs totaled $45.195 billion. That figure amounts to a total *increase* in spending on international affairs during President Obama's second year in office—with the approval of a Democrat majority in both houses of Congress—of 163% *above* the Clinton Administration's level of spending for the year 2000, and an increase of 57% over what the Bush Administration spend in 2008, President Bush's last year in office.

We all can recognize that it is vitally important for the United States to cultivate and maintain friendly relationships with our foreign allies and trading partners, and to fully support our State Department's diplomats and embassies in all four corners of the globe. But what kind of bookkeeping madness can possibly justify increasing spending by more than two-and-one-half times during a brief ten years span in the midst of our own economic hardship? No private enterprise—no matter how large—could long survive such gross mismanagement.

In 2008, the Bush Administration spent a total of $23.8 billion on foreign aid around the world. America's "assistance to developing countries" included Afghanistan, Iraq, the Sudan, the Palestinian-Administered Areas, Ethiopia, Colombia, Pakistan, Kenya, South African, Jordan, Uganda, Nigeria, Haiti, Tanzania, Georgia, Mozambique, Zimbabwe, the Democratic Republic of the Congo, Zambia, and Cote d'Ivoire. In 2009, the Obama Administration, in spite of America's fiscal crisis, *increased* U.S. assistance payments to these and other developing countries by an additional $1.3 billion.

The United States is a charitable and noble nation. We Americans share an almost missionary zeal for helping destitute countries around the world. We can rightfully be proud of our long tradition of offering government and private assistance wherever our fellow human beings are suffering. Our humanitarian relief efforts following global disasters are legendary. But even we Americans have limits on what we can afford.

Going broke while helping the world's poor may be noble, but how does that help us Americans to provide "social justice" for the poor and homeless, the ill and handicapped, here at home? Whatever happened to the old saying, "Charity begins at home"? And where will all those extra dollars to provide for "social justice" here at home come from? Beijing?

Chapter 5

....

FEDERAL JUSTICE

Speaking of "justice," in 2010, the Obama Administration spent $53.4 billion on the "Administration of Justice" for federal law enforcement activities, federal courts and litigation costs, federal prisons, and criminal justice assistance. 53.4 billion for 2010 was an 88% *increase* over what the Clinton Administration spent on the administration of justice in 2000, and a 13% increase over President Bush's top spending year, 2008. In 2008, 47.1 billion was spent on the judicial branch of our federal government. In 2009, 51.5 billion was spent, and in 2010, 53.4 billion. The annual cost of our federal judiciary nearly doubled from 2000 ($28.5 billion) to 2010 ($53.4 billion).

Are we Americans experiencing some sort of crime wave of federal criminal offenses? Or might the 88% increase in judicial costs be associated with stricter enforcement of our federal immigration laws?

According to recent Federal Bureau of Investigation (FBI) *Uniform Crime Reports*, which are published annually, crime in the United States had steadily *declined* per every 1,000 residents in nearly every category of crimes reported. That is good news. In addition, most crimes committed in the United Stares each year are violations of *state*, not federal, laws, and are therefore adjudicated in state-funded courts. For example, at the end of 2009, the total number of inmates held in American prisons, as reported by the FBI, was 1,613,740. Of that number, only 208,118 were held in federal prisons at year's end. State prisons in each of the following states rivaled the entire federal penitentiary system in total numbers of inmates as of December 31, 2009, according to the U.S. Department of Justice, Bureau of Justice statistics: California (171,274), Texas (171,249), Florida (103,915), and New York (58,687). In 2009, those four states along housed 505,126 inmates at state expense, or more than double federal totals for the entire United States.

Back to the federal justice system. In the year 2000, the federal government spent approximately $3,707,000,000 on the incarceration of 145,416 prisoners in federal penitentiaries, at an average cost of $25,492.38. In 2010, federal prisons housed 208,118 inmates at an approximate total cost of $7,748,000,000. When comparing the federal prison population of 2000 with 2010, both the size of the prison population *and* the cost per prisoner increased over ten years by thirty-one percent. But the total expenditure on federal prisons more than doubled between 2000 and 2010. Why? Are we making our federal prisons "green"?

Chapter 6

. . . .

"GREEN ENERGY"

As most of us Americans surely know by now, "green energy," as opposed to the burning of coal and petroleum products, is reported to be environmentally friendly. The Obama Administration, in concert with its Environmental Protection Agency (EPA), has placed increasing emphasis on both new anti-pollution regulations for American industry, and has also provided federal loans and grants for the development and manufacture of new "green energy" products, especially in such areas as solar energy and wind power.[6]

---

[6]   The EPA was first established by President Richard Nixon in January 1970 to help clean up America's environment.

While the EPA has been in existence since 1970, large federal expenditures on private ventures to produce "green energy" products are unique to the Obama Administration. For example, in 2000, the Clinton Administration spent approximately 1.6 billion on "energy." The Bush Administration spent 1.4 billion in 2005 on energy, 1.1 billion in 2007, and 1.0 billion in 2008. In 2009, by contrast, the Obama Administration spent 4.75 billion on green energy, a 375% increase over the previous year. And, in 2010, the Obama Administration spent an additional 11.6 billion on matters relating to green energy, bringing the total spending on energy appropriations for the administration's first two years to a whopping 16.35 billions in taxpayer dollars.

In order to ease the pain, such *spending* has been called "investing." Unfortunately, when our national debt is over *sixteen trillion dollars*, how can we Americans afford to "invest" *or* spend over 1000% more than we have in the past? Call it "investing," or call it "spending," we as a people and as a nation are still shelling out far more than we make, hour by hour, day by day. Green energy may be good for us, but not if the price is bankruptcy and financial ruin.

On January 23, 1996, President Bill Clinton addressed a packed House Chamber during his *State of the Union Address*. In one of the most famous—*and popular*—statements of his entire presidency, Mr. Clinton declared that "the era of big government is over." The applause from both Democrats and Republicans in that chamber was thunderous. Was Clinton wrong?

Chapter 7

....

BIG GOVERNMENT

Sixteen years have passed since President Bill Clinton's second inauguration was held on America's newest national holiday—Martin Luther King Day, January 20, 1997. On that day, in his *Second Inaugural Address*, President Clinton advised his fellow Americans that "We need a new government for a new century—humble enough not to try to solve all our problems for us . . . a government that is smaller, lives within its means, and does more with less."

Now, only sixteen years later, President Clinton's pragmatic vision for America has become transformed into a big, bumbling, and regressive bureaucracy mired in a long-ago discredited mind-set of *central planning* in Washington, D.C., *for the greater good*. As Ronald Reagan once said in response to a statement by Jimmy Carter, "There you go again!" But this time, the you is *we*. *We* are likely headed towards a financial disaster as we follow our Pied-Piper-In-Chief. If only President Obama had followed Clinton's advice—or even Reagan's, or Eisenhower's—and tried to do *more with less*, we would surely be in less of a mess today.

We already know that our national debt is currently $16.4 trillion and growing by the minute. And we have learned that each of us Americans—every man, woman, and child—already owes more than $110,000 in federal debt (not counting our own personal debts). But do we Americans know how gigantic our federal bureaucracy has already become? Here is one truly frightening statistic for you: Our Department of Defense, which accounts for less than twenty percent of our annual federal expenditures, has more *civilian* employees (734,065 in 2009, according to the U.S. Office of Personnel Management) than our entire U.S. Postal Service (688,582 in 2009). And that is just the tip of the iceberg. By 2009, the *executive branch* of our federal government had grown to 1,880,134 civilian employees plus 1,466,974 active duty military personnel.

That same year, 2009, the *legislative branch* of our federal government, including all 435 members of the House of Representatives and 100 Senators, employed a total of 29,933 people. And our *judicial branch*, including the nine justices of our Supreme Court, employed a total of 33,754-483 for the Supreme Court and 33,271 for all other federal courts.

Taken all together, in 2009, our federal government employed a grand total of 3,410,795 active civilian and military personnel. According to the 2010 U.S. Census, the total population of the United States that year was 308,745,538. Of those 308,745,538 persons living in the United States in 2010, 74,165,365 were 17 years of age or younger (24% of the total population), and an additional 40,433,525 were 65 years of age or older (13.1% of the total population). Assuming that the remaining 62.9% of the population comprises America's "work force," nearly two out of every one hundred age-eligible Americans works in some capacity for our federal government. And, keep in mind, that does not include those millions of Americans who work for state governments, city and county governments, public school districts, community colleges, and public universities across our nation. Is government *big* today, and growing *bigger*? You bet!

Is the trend towards a growing federal bureaucracy with ever-increasing numbers of civilian employees earning higher average salaries, medical and dental benefits, and retirement guarantees than our shrinking private business sector can afford to pay (except for Wall Street executives and professional athletes) making America a better place for all of us to live? Has a weakening desire on the part of millions of Americans to remain self-sufficient resulted in their increased dependence on the federal government for economic assistance? Are Food Stamps more popular now than ever before? Has the Food Stamp Program (now known as "SNAP"—the Supplemental Nutrition Assistance Program) really *increased* in size from $15.4 million in 1990 to $68.3 million by 2010?

Way back in 1968, the eminent historians Will and Ariel Durant concluded rather prophetically in their classic book, *The Lessons of History*, that "The fear of capitalism has compelled socialism to widen freedom, and the fear of socialism has compelled capitalism to increase equality. East is West and West is East, and soon the twain will meet."[7] The Durant's 1968 prophecy may help explain why today's Communist China, certainly once more restrictive of entrepreneurial endeavors due to the ideology of Chairman Mao than even the most socialistic of European countries, now allows privately-owned businesses in such booming commercial centers as Shanghai and Hong Kong to *exist and flourish virtually unrestricted*—as long as the political leadership of the Communist Party remains unopposed. Why? China's communist leaders have come to recognize, after years of trial and error, that *capitalism, private ownership* of the means of production, distribution, and exchange of goods, is the most efficient *solution* to the economic problems of modern industrialized nations. Besides, entrepreneurism, prior to the 20th Century communist movement in China, was a tradition in China for thousands of years. For many centuries, Chinese entrepreneurs were *the* merchants of Asia. And, as late as 1776, China was more prosperous

---

[7]   Will and Ariel Durant, *The Lessons of History* (New York: Simon & Schuster, 1968), p. 67.

than *all* of Europe. As long as the merchants of Asia paid occasional tribute to the Emperor and his Celestial Court, they were free to do pretty much as they pleased. And China prospered. As China is surely doing again today under her modern emperors.

Meanwhile, ignoring the lessons of history past and present, and in apparent fulfillment of the Durant's 1968 prophecy for the West, the Obama Administration continues to embrace *central economic planning* as "Forward Looking," *wealth redistribution* as the key to "social justice," and *Keynesian economics* as the spending path to prosperity. How absurd!

The roots of capitalism can be found whenever free men came together, utilized their talents and common sense, and conducted business without the interference of government. Capitalism, the "free-enterprise system," is based upon *freedom of choice*. Since freedom of choice is inherent in a democracy, historically, capitalism has found its strongest home in America. America was founded by capitalists—English businessmen who came to Jamestown in 1607 in search of profits in the new "land of opportunity." Since our early colonial beginnings, farms, workshops, foundries, stores, etc., have been the private property of individuals or companies, at times protected but rarely regulated by government. It is because of our capitalistic roots—our "free-enterprise system"—that America came to enjoy the highest standard of living the world has ever known. Historically, we Americans have long pursued *equality of opportunity*, not *equality of condition*. Equality of condition, or "social justice," has long been the ultimate goal of socialistic "humanitarians" in those societies of the past that idealistically sought "economic equality." Like it or not, equality of opportunity has trumped equality of condition, or "economic equality," time and time again. The two best modern-day examples of the superiority of "free-enterprise" over "central planning" and "shared wealth" is the collapse of the Soviet Empire under Mikhail Gorbachev and the dramatic economic transformation of Communist China after the death of Chairman Mao.

America was founded on *common sense*. It is too bad there is so little common sense roaming the corridors of power in our nation's capital today. For example, show me the common sense involved in *spending more* to avoid bankruptcy. Isn't over-spending the very same reason our federal government is going broke in the first place? Would it not make more sense to *reduce* spending rather than *increase* it?

The average American today is also sorely lacking in common sense when it comes to the federal government. How else can we explain why we continue to allow a few "central planners" in Washington, D.C., to dictate to the more than 300 million of us what we can and can not do, from the kinds of light bulbs and toilets we use in our own private homes, to the quality of medical care we may—*and may not*—receive.

Currently, the two largest nations in the world, China and India, are both loosening their past practices of central control over their economies while encouraging entrepreneurship and free-enterprise. The results so far? Millions of Chinese and Indians have risen out of poverty to become middle class, and many have even become wealthy as others strive to join them. Isn't that the *American way?*

Meanwhile, in America, we appear to be headed in the opposite direction—away from self-reliance and entrepreneurship and onto the same failed path the East once followed. Our charismatic Pied-Piper-in-Chief, Barack Obama, is leading us "Forward!" to central planning and wealth redistribution. These are the same old tired promises once uttered tongue-in-cheek by Stalin and Mao. President Barack Obama claims he is not a socialist. I take him at his word. President Obama is certainly charismatic, and he appears to be well-intentioned. Unfortunately, by his own economic record while in office, he seems to lack an essential characteristic our great nation was founded upon—*common sense*. May freedom and common sense replace the "Nanny State" before it is too late.

BIBLIOGRAPHY

Ambrose, Stephen E. *Eisenhower: Soldier and President*. New York: Simon & Schuster, 1991.

Boller, Paul F., Jr. *Presidential Campaigns: From George Washington to George W. Bush*. New York: Oxford University Press, 2004.

Chung, Jung, and John Halliday. *Mao: The Unknown Story*. New York: Alfred A Knopf, 2005.

D'Souza, Dinesh. *Obama's America: Unmaking the American Dream*. New York: Regnery Publishing, Inc., 2012.

Durant, Will and Ariel. *The Lessons of History*. New York: Simon & Schuster, 1968.

Friedman, Milton & Rose. *Free to Choose*. New York: Harcourt Brace Jovanovich, 1979.

Goodwin, Doris Kearns. *Lyndon Johnson and the American Dream*. New York: St. Martin's Press, 1991.

Hamilton, Nigel. *Bill Clinton: Mastering the Presidency*. New York: Perseus Books, 2007.

Hayward, Steven F. *The Age of Reagan*. New York: Crown Forum, 2009.

Kennedy, Paul. *The Rise and Fall of the Great Powers: Economic Change and Military Conflict from 1500 to 2000*. New York: Random House, 1986.

Kissinger, Henry. *On China*. New York: The Penguin Press, 2011.

McCullough, David. *Truman*. New York: Broadway Books, 2006.

Newton, Jim. *Eisenhower: The White House Years*. New York: Doubleday, 2011.

O'Reilly, Bill. *Culture Warrior*. New York: Simon & Schuster, 1992.

Sebestyen, Victor. *Revolution 1989: The Fall of the Soviet Empire*. New York: Pantheon Books, 2009.

Stanley, Richard T. *Lessons of American History*. New York: iUniverse, 2007.

Thomas, Evan. *Ike's Bluff: President Eisenhower's Secret Battle to Save the World*. New York: Little, Brown and Company, 2012.

Woodward, Bob. *Bush at War*. New York: Simon & Schuster, 2002.

www.ingramcontent.com/pod-product-compliance
Lightning Source LLC
Chambersburg PA
CBHW020403290526
45785CB00005B/2426

* 9 7 8 1 4 7 5 9 7 4 3 0 0 *